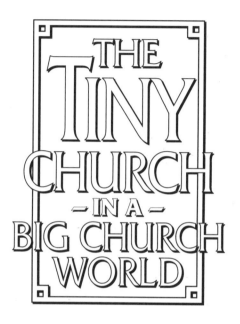

THE
TINY
CHURCH
– IN A –
BIG CHURCH
WORLD

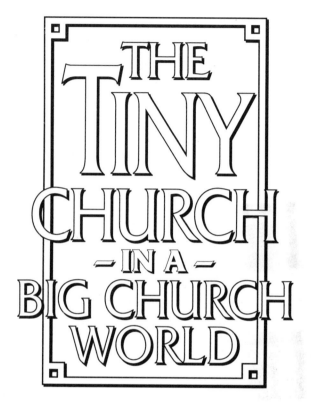

THE TINY CHURCH -IN A- BIG CHURCH WORLD

Richard P. Thompson

NAZARENE PUBLISHING HOUSE
Kansas City, Missouri

Contents

98191

Introduction

Perhaps the problem was not as big as it seemed to her, but I told her I would see what I could do. She was working with children in the church's missionary emphasis, and she felt we needed more materials for the monthly Sunday evening services to make them meaningful to the children. With a sense of uncertainty, I made a telephone call to our church headquarters in Kansas City. To my surprise, the person on the other end was in partial agreement and in complete sympathy with our children's missions worker. He believed that the problem was a simple one, though the solutions were not so. In our determination to teach children about our mission work, we had included a fairly wide range of ages. The headquarters employee explained that in such a group, children from three to nine years of age, the differences in interest and ability were very distinct. The problem, then, was not in the curriculum materials we were using, but that the age span was too broad to make it enjoyable and beneficial for each child. Our desires were notable; our purposes were admirable. Our error was in seeing children as one general group, inadvertently ignoring distinctive characteristics of each age-group.

The same kind of subtle error or oversight happens when we "look" at churches. In church growth circles, a small church is defined as "a church that averages 200 or less in a typical service." For some churches, this would apply to Sunday School; for others, the morning worship would be a more appropriate gauge; for still others, the membership total would be the best measure for categorization. This definition would seem adequate, since a church of 200 would have more in common with a church of 50 than with a church of 1,000. Reality, however, tells us differently. To the "tiny" congregation of 25 or 30, 200 seems large.[1]

The grouping of all churches of 200 or less into one category ignores some distinct qualities, dynamics, and concerns of more specific groupings. To attempt to provide identical resources and reference manuals for all churches in the "small church" category misses the mark, as we did with the problem of children in our missions service. Lyle Schaller, an expert in church studies, said,

> The congregation averaging less than 35 or 40 at worship can be represented by an acorn squash, the church averaging 125 at worship can be depicted by a pumpkin, the congregation averaging 200 at worship might be portrayed by a horse, and a huge church averaging 500 or 600 or more at worship can be symbolized by a fifteen-room house. . . . They are almost as different from one another as a village is unlike a large central city. . . . The person who is very competent in raising pumpkins may not be an expert at caring for horses. The fifteen-room house requires both maintenance and a different kind of care than the garden in which one raises squash and pumpkins. A different perspective and a different set of criteria should be used in grading squash or pumpkins that would be used in judging a horse or appraising a large house. . . . The small church is different. Recognize and affirm those differences![2]

In his book titled *Small Churches Are the Right Size*, David R. Ray states:

> The small church is *not* a prepubescent, immature, dwarfed, or malnourished large church. Because of its different size and resulting different nature . . . it will look different, feel different, act differently, be different.[3]

If these men are correct in comparing the small church to

the large church, the same principles would apply in comparing the tiny church with the small church.

Perhaps we need a breakdown of the "small church" category. In so doing materials and resources can be prepared with their specific needs in mind. A separate category for the smallest of churches is a start in the right direction. Any person who has participated in what we call a tiny church will acknowledge its unique qualities and problems. Unfortunately, many times the problems either are allowed to overwhelm and overshadow the good dynamics of the setting, or they are not dealt with effectively. In these cases, the tiny church becomes locked into a cycle that inhibits growth.

This is not always the case. There are many tiny churches where God is blessing and working in people's lives, although the gains may seem minimal in comparison to the larger churches around them. An inherent danger can arise from earnest efforts to copy what the larger churches are doing, rather than acknowledging their distinctive traits.

The tiny church must work effectively within its circumstances, as well as deal honestly with issues unique to it. If the tiny church tries to function on the basis of principles for small churches in general, the results will often be frustration and discouragement. That need not be the case, for they worship the same God as the people in larger churches and are accessed by the same Holy Spirit who empowers others. Expectancy and excitement are found in tiny churches as well as in large ones. The secret is in their living and working within their unique traits so that they will be more effective as a vital center of evangelism and ministry.

The tiny church is more common than most people realize. Some statistics will help to clarify this. In the United States the Church of the Nazarene (as reported in the statistics from the 1986-87 church year)[4] had 5,027 churches and church-type missions. Of these, approximately 4,416 were considered, by church growth standards, small churches. However, it is noteworthy to observe the groupings of these small churches in more definitive categories:

MEMBERSHIP	NO. OF CHURCHES	% OF CHURCHES
1-25	655	13.03
26-50	1,133	22.54
51-75	904	17.98
76-200	1,724	34.29

SUN. SCHOOL AVG. ATTEND.	NO. OF CHURCHES	% OF CHURCHES
1-25	782	15.56
26-50	1,408	28.01
51-75	940	18.70
76-200	1,526	30.36

A.M. WORSHIP AVG. ATTEND.	NO. OF CHURCHES	% OF CHURCHES
1-25	649	12.91
26-50	1,259	25.04
51-75	926	18.42
76-200	1,642	32.66

It is apparent, based upon these facts, that approximately two-thirds of small churches in the Church of the Nazarene are in the "75 or less" category. In fact, the largest percentage of these are in the "50 or less" grouping, the tiny church.

The statistics from the 1987-88 church year for the Washington District of the Church of the Nazarene also yield similar findings.[5] From a total of 75 churches on the district, we find the following:

MEMBERSHIP	NO. OF CHURCHES	% OF CHURCHES
1-25	4	5.3
26-50	15	20.0
51-75	18	24.0
76-200	26	34.7

SUN. SCHOOL AVG. ATTEND.	NO. OF CHURCHES	% OF CHURCHES
1-25	12	16.0
26-50	17	22.7
51-75	18	24.0
76-200	21	28.0

A.M. WORSHIP AVG. ATTEND.	NO. OF CHURCHES	% OF CHURCHES
1-25	7	9.3
26-50	20	26.7
51-75	13	17.3
76-200	28	37.3

These Washington District statistics agree with those of the denomination as to natural groupings of churches. One church size that has the potential for making strides in reaching out to our world in the name of our Lord is the church of 50 or less, the tiny church. Church growth materials and how-to books tend to deal more with the 75-200 group in the small church category. Therefore, it seems reasonable to give added attention to the 50-or-less category.

The main focus of this work is to those who are a part of a tiny church—the pastor (especially the new pastor who usually finds himself in this setting), the lay leaders, the ministry directors, and the church board. For many tiny churches, a small handful of dedicated and committed people fill all these positions. It is hoped that the people of the tiny church will be able to see their viability and recognize the potential service for God. The desire is that they will be assisted in strategic areas of their large task in a tiny setting. May the tiny church of which they are a part become excited by their vision for the future, as they work together in the name of Jesus Christ, as they sense the possibilities that are uniquely theirs as a body of Christ in their particular setting. But it is also intended that ministry leaders in other churches (pastors and laymen alike) will develop a sense of awareness, assistance, and shared vision for the tiny sister church near them.

The topics and principles dealt with here are presented in a somewhat logical sequence, though it may be that a different order may be required by circumstances in particular settings. For example, a church's self-perception may be affected by their financial condition, or evangelistic efforts may be affected by misplaced priorities. Flexibility in approaching these differing situations is essential. But sequence is not the matter of importance—help and results are!

1

Just Because We Are Tiny Does Not Mean We Are a Failure

We hear a lot about the importance of self-esteem today. Basically, it is that our perception of ourselves as persons has a lot to do with what we become. Maslow would tell us that we cannot reach self-actualization unless we have a proper self-image. If that is true for individuals, would this not also be true for a group of persons who have joined themselves together as the Body of Christ? Is it not safe to assume that the perception a church has of itself will affect its self-actualization as a continuation of the earthly ministry of our Lord?

But what about the tiny church? How do the members of the tiny church see themselves? Largely, the tiny church suffers from low morale as a result of a low self-perception. David R. Ray states,

> A large problem of many small churches is low morale. By osmosis they have picked up from the culture and larger church the feeling that they are insignificant because they are small. In relation to the world around, small-church people do not get much ego, status, and esteem satisfaction.[1]

If that is true for the small church, one can imagine what the problem is for the "smaller of the small" churches. Because one of the by-products of our American culture is a concern with bigness, a common assumption is that smallness is wrong by nature. As a result, new people in the community may not give the tiny church an opportunity to minister to them. In addition, members in small churches frequently feel they are neglected, forgotten, or, even worse, looked down upon within their own denomination.

This feeling is reinforced in a number of ways. One way is in the reporting of statistics. The churches with the largest numbers in increased attendance or giving are often listed in the denominational publications while many times the tiny church that has the greater percentage growth is ignored. At annual district assemblies, it is difficult for the tiny church to compete with the churches with multiple ministries. The exciting news is all about the great increases and programs of the larger churches.

A third intimidation is in the denominational programming that is designed for the larger settings and cannot possibly be used in the tiny ones. When these all come together in the minds of the people of the tiny church, it is sometimes difficult to feel excited and significant. Thus, there is low morale and a feeling of unworthiness.

This common perception of people about their tiny church is not helped by persons such as James L. Lowery, Jr., who states emphatically that the small church, or, in this case, the tiny church, is not viable because of its size, which makes it "unable to be very Christian."[2] What must be seen is that the tiny church, regardless of the opinions of others, is not necessarily tiny because it has failed. In fact, the persons of the tiny church may see themselves as possessing a wonderful opportunity to fulfill the Great Commission of our Lord, even in their "tininess." The tininess of a church does not necessarily condemn it to being a failure any more than the largeness of another church proclaims it a success. What does determine failure or success is the choice of the church itself. The church can choose to view itself as a failure or as a vital part of the kingdom of God, with wonderful possibilities for sharing the love and grace of God with others.

Consider Your Setting

What can help the tiny church when failure seems to be the common perception? Let's consider three things. First, **consider your location.** Is there a large or limited population? Are people moving in or moving away rapidly? Are there other churches, either of your denomination or others, that attract members from your church because they have more to offer? What is the overall condition of the church concerning vision, morale, finance, and other factors? All of these influence possible growth for the tiny church. What must be remembered is that the setting of the church—its location, its condition—has a profound impact upon its growth, and therefore its size. There are times when faithfulness will not yield visible fruitfulness. But the church cannot rest in these times for long.

Consider Your Accomplishments

A second suggestion is to **consider your accomplishments.** Too often we focus on failures rather than on success. It is easier to see the smallness and the limitations than it is to see the accomplishments and possibilities. If the church is indeed Christian, then its successes should serve as a source of encouragement. Of course, the inherent danger is that if people look back too long, they lose proper perspective. And yet when failure seems real, the people of the tiny church need to see that they too have been effective in the ministry of Jesus Christ—that person whose life was transformed in a radical way; that person who left the church to prepare for full-time Christian service; the numerous persons who are now members of churches across the nation who were nurtured and grew within the fellowship of the church. It could even be the successful building of the church facility. It is good to look back from time to time, for in looking back, one can see the fingerprints of God on the months and years. When the people of the tiny church can see that God has been at work in their midst as well as in the larger churches, they will not be so apt to see themselves as failures—because they aren't!

Consider Your Attitudes

In his book titled *Your Attitude: Key to Success,* John Maxwell gives seven axioms concerning attitudes:

1. Our attitude determines our approach to life.
2. Our attitude determines our relationships with people.
3. Often our attitude is the only difference between success and failure.
4. Our attitude at the beginning of a task will affect its outcome more than anything else.
5. Our attitude can turn our problems into blessings.
6. Our attitude can give us an uncommonly positive perspective.
7. Our attitude is not automatically good just because we are Christians.[3]

These same axioms may be applied to the church as well. There are some things that we simply cannot control as persons. There are some things that we cannot control as a church. But the church can control, with the guidance and help of the Holy Spirit, much of what happens within it. Part of this has to do with the attitudes. When we choose to see ourselves as insignificant and of little influence and effectiveness, our negative attitudes and self-images become self-fulfilling prophecies. But we can choose to see ourselves in a different light—anticipating possibilities, expecting the best, never allowing failures to become final. The tiny church is not a failure because it is tiny; it is only a failure when it settles for failure.

Though all these axioms could be applied to the church, let us examine just two. The third axiom states, "Often our attitude is the only difference between success and failure." The reason for this is simple: there is little difference between success and failure. Many times we only need to change a little to see success in our efforts for Christ. The following illustrates this principle:

Although the numbers
only increases by one $4 \times 4 \times 4 \times 4 = 256$
each, the total increases $5 \times 5 \times 5 \times 5 = 625$
by nearly 250%.

It may be that the tiny church, tempted to feel like a failure, is actually close to success in its efforts to grow. The church may be close to realizing its vision for its ministry. Or perhaps it is only one small step away in several areas that will cause it to be a model of faithfulness *and* increased fruitfulness. Don't see your church as being close to failure; see how close you are to success in terms of being the vital, exciting, and growing Body of Christ you hope to be.

The fourth axiom is also pertinent for the church— "Our attitude at the beginning of a task will affect its outcome more than anything else." If that is true for the church, then we must ask ourselves this: Do we see ourselves as failures, or as winners? Do we see ourselves as disciples of Jesus Christ on a mission to spread the gospel? Or do we see ourselves as disciples who cannot make much of a difference in our community because we are so small? If we see ourselves as failures, we can go out with confidence—we will fail! If we see ourselves as being very limited because of size, then the results will likely be limited. But if we see the opportunities before us, and if we have the power of the Holy Spirit to enable us, we can expect to see God at work through us and in us. We have heard the old saying, "All's well that ends well." Instead of that, we can say, "All's well that begins well . . . in Christ."[4] The key is in our attitude toward ourselves and toward our mission.

The tiny church's self-perception is significant. Too many tiny churches have defeated themselves unnecessarily. It is not because they are disobedient or because they do not want to grow or even because they do not care about others. It is because they simply *see* themselves as failures. But failure is not determined by largeness or smallness, or even by the successes a church can claim for itself. Neither is failure determined by how one church measures up to other churches and ministries. Failure is final when hope is gone, when concern is lost, when effort is diminished. If your desire is to fulfill in your community the Great Commission for the church, then your tiny church is not a failure. If your desire is to be Christ to those who do not know Him, then your tiny church is not a failure. If you are being used by God to touch the lives of others with His love, then your tiny church is not a failure. Those whom God uses are not losers, but winners! Not failures, but successes! Our Heavenly Father has big dreams for His people in the tiny church.

Just because we are tiny does not mean we are a failure.

2

Our Purpose Determines Our Priorities

An old saying goes something like this: "If you aim at nothing, you will hit it every time." Absolutely correct! If we strive to accomplish nothing, we will accomplish nothing. If we set out with no real purpose for living, then we probably will not find much fulfillment in life. And this simple principle holds true in many areas of life.

Let's consider baseball. We are told that baseball is a "game of inches." A baseball may hit the top of the outfield wall or may be a home run, with only an inch making the difference. The difference of an inch may determine whether a baseball is hit solidly or is only a grounder. That is why hitting coaches and fielding instructors remind their players to keep their eye on the ball. If the eyes leave the baseball for only a moment, chances are the player will not succeed in hitting the ball cleanly or in fielding the ball flawlessly. The focus of the player will determine, to a large degree, his ability to successfully accomplish his task.

Intention vs. Attention

Many times our churches do not "keep their eye on the ball." It is not that the churches want to fail; it is not that churches have made a decision to be unfaithful to God or to be disobedient or to be unfruitful. In most cases, churches do not make conscious decisions to hinder effectiveness. Our concern is not about **intention;** our concern is about **attention** and how it is directed. What we need to remember is that the church and individuals alike have a purpose of one sort or another. That which demands our attention, that which becomes a priority with us, reflects our true purpose, because our purpose determines our priorities. This is true for the megachurch, the large church, the small church, and the tiny church. All churches have a documented or implied purpose as seen in the priorities of their ministries.

Purpose Can Be Too Small

The tiny church is particularly vulnerable at this point. Because of its unique characteristics, there may be a tendency to succumb to purposes that are as small as the church. One such tendency is to focus, at least unconsciously, upon survival. Unlike other churches, the tiny church must deal with the possibility of death. But in the process, Paul O. Madsen states,

> The church often turns inward in such situations in an attempt to perpetuate itself. It thus increases its own problem because it has no energy or time for evangelism, social action, and community interest. It becomes a tight, little enclave which seeks desperately, or even worse, seeks haphazardly for solutions to institutional problems of budget, leadership, and program. The focus is wrong. Theologically, the church should be turned outward. Its concern must always be for the world created by God. But in its own illness, it is struggling to keep the lifeblood moving within its own body and has no strength left for those outside its own small body. It has not learned the spiritual truth that Jesus enunciated so long ago, "that he who would find his life must lose it." The church struggles instead to preserve its own life and in the end may die, for its focus has become material and not spiritual.[1]

Without realizing it, the tiny church may actually be functioning with a purpose of survival. This is not to say that survival is wrong in nature. Bills must be paid, the needs of the pastoral family must be provided for, and ministries must be accomplished. Resources are needed to continue ministry. But when survival becomes the dominant theme, the problem is not one of lack of purpose, but of **too small a purpose.** When this happens, the church is functioning and focusing on something smaller than the promises and desires of God.

The survival of the church is essential; otherwise, there is no ministry. Thus survival is a challenging and motivating factor and should not be seen as negative in nature. But survival must not overshadow the *real purpose* for that church. There is a difference between a healthy and challenging purpose on the one hand, and a small purpose on the other. What we need to remember in the tiny church is that "we fail, not because of big problems, but because of small purposes."[2]

If we look to the story of David and Goliath (1 Samuel 17), we find that our failures are not caused by giant problems that we confront. It is not the Goliaths that defeat us, but small purposes. If our purpose is small, our priorities will be small in comparison to the wondrous love and grace of God for the lives of all mankind.

Purposes Can Be Too Broad

There is another point of vulnerability for the tiny church. Just as a small purpose can be a source of difficulty, so can **too broad a purpose** be detrimental. If the purpose is too broad, then the church is pulled in too many directions.

Too broad a purpose is characterized by **inclusiveness.** Some churches try to include everything good as part of their mission for Christ, most of which would have a valid claim in the worldwide mission of the universal Church. But much of it would be beyond the scope of a single church.

In addition, broad purposes are often characterized by **vagueness,** or lack of specificity. The results are much like that of inclusiveness. Vagueness may lead to a broad outlook in the purpose of the church, ending in a scattering of resources and emphases. This causes the persons of the church to focus in directions that may not be totally aligned with one another. The sense of cohesiveness in effort and mission is hindered if not lost, and the effectiveness of the church in specific areas is limited.

This is a potential problem for the largest church as well as the smallest. It must be stated, however, that the problems are more severe for the tiny church. Because of the lack of resources, whether in terms of people or finances, the tiny church simply cannot afford to be pulled in too many directions. It can be difficult to cover some of the basics, let alone other opportunities for ministry.

There must be a sense of conservation on the part of the church in relation to its purpose. No effort or money can be wasted. The purpose of the church must be specific enough that it will give godly direction to the people, yet within it must be the flexibility for increased opportunities for ministry as it grows and as resources become available. A clear understanding and statement of purpose must be developed that is specific on the one hand and yet inclusive enough "to include every action in which the church is involved."[3]

Purpose and Priorities

The purpose of the church, therefore, will determine the priorities of the church. It is easy to see that vision begins with, and is passed on in many ways by, the stated purpose of a church. A great purpose will motivate people to give their energy, effort, time, and commitment—THEMSELVES. It will keep the church and its people from giving up, even in tough times. It puts "seasoning" in the life of the church and makes it "tasty and exciting."[4] It is this purpose that will lift the church out of the realm of the ordinary and will cause the people to

P Pray more than ordinary people
U Unite more than ordinary people
R Risk more than ordinary people
P Plan more than ordinary people
O Observe more than ordinary people
S Sacrifice more than ordinary people
E Expect more than ordinary people[5]

A common sense of purpose will not happen by accident. It occurs when the people of a church join together to discover their Christian direction as the Body of Christ. It may be that the statement of purpose will be a definitive one such as the following:

> **The purpose of the church is to glorify God by making disciples of all nations through the continued ministry of Jesus in worship, evangelism, discipleship, fellowship, and mercy.[6]**

Or it may be something that is more memorable such as:

> **As a dynamic church proclaiming the Word of God we purpose to make disciples of Christ by:**
> > **Exalting God**
> > **Encouraging Christians**
> > **Equipping Christians**
> > **Evangelizing the World[7]**

> **The purpose of the church is to make disciples of our community by focusing upon the life of Christian holiness as exemplified by Jesus Christ through T.L.C.:**
> > **Together Lifting up Christ**
> > **Together Learning about Christ**
> > **Together Loving like Christ**
> > **Together Leading others to Christ[8]**

What is important is that a church's stated purpose be that which describes, for the people of that particular church, the reason for their existence, defining for them what direction their church should go—what their church will be like. There are at least seven reasons for developing a statement of purpose:

1. A stated purpose will motivate the church.

2. A stated purpose will keep the church's priorities straight.
3. A stated purpose will develop the church's potential.
4. A stated purpose will give the church power to live in the present.
5. A stated purpose will produce high morale.
6. A stated purpose will help the church minister more effectively.
7. A stated purpose will help the church evaluate its progress.[9]

Such a statement of purpose can only come about when the people work together to define their reason for existence. To be effective and give guidance, a statement of purpose must be, among other things,

1. Biblical
2. Definitive
3. Concise
4. Memorable
5. Personal
6. Challenging

It is important for every church, regardless of its size or its distinctives, to define its purpose. For the tiny church, however, the purpose may have an even greater impact upon its ministries and its potential growth. The tiny church need not have a tiny purpose! God's grace and power are available, and He can and will work in any church that strives to fulfill the mission He has for it.

Our purpose determines our priorities.

3

Set Realistic Goals

A declaration of purpose is especially important for the tiny church. The smaller the church, the easier it is to become sidetracked by smaller purposes. The tiny church simply cannot afford to be diverted from its central mission. Because there are not sufficient resources to focus on several interests or directions, a realistic statement of purpose is essential, keeping before the small congregation its reason for existence.

Included in this process is the establishment of goals. It is one thing to have a purpose, but that purpose will never become anything more than a good statement unless it is lived out through goals. The purpose is like a skeleton, and the goals are the flesh. Goals, properly developed, will bring the church to realize in increasing measure their statement of purpose. The purpose, then, is what the church desires to be as the body of Christ; the goals are the steps that lead them to the fulfillment of their purpose.

All churches, from the smallest to the largest, would benefit from a list of goals. In fact, whether it is an individual, a business, or an institution, most are better off with a clear set of goals. The need and advantage for careful goal setting by the tiny church is even greater because of its vulnerability to problems created by either the lack of goals or the establishment of inadequate ones. These may not be *the* cause of ineffectiveness but a contributing factor. However, careful goal setting by the tiny church may be significant in accomplishing fruitful and effective service in God's kingdom.

Let us focus on five particular characteristics of goals that can help the tiny church:

G Guiding
O Optimistic
A Attainable
L Lay-developed
S Specific

Guiding Goals

Goals should give guidance, leading the church toward fulfillment of their purpose. This is particularly important for the tiny church in light of the smaller amount of available resources. There are fewer people, less funds, less tools with which to enhance ministry and program opportunities. But that will not be a source of defeat or frustration if their goals help them work with what is available. Goals involve planning and effort and require looking into the future, focusing on the purpose of the church. The process "involves determining what should and can be done to achieve a future that is desirable and to help avoid a future that is not desirable but would occur if we do nothing."[1] The reason for this is very simple: "to help accomplish the most meaningful and rewarding results for our church. We do this by:

1. determining the most important things (goals) we want to reach;
2. directing all of the individual efforts toward accomplishing these goals; and
3. avoiding spending time and effort on activities which are not needed."[2]

In the tiny church, it is all we can handle to provide some of the basics of ministry. Thus a conscious decision to implement goals will help everyone focus on essentials, guiding them to fulfillment of their Christ-given mission.

Optimistic Goals

The church as an institution has come into being because of its faith—faith in the grace of God through our Lord and Savior, Jesus Christ. This faith draws us together to worship God, to learn more about Him, and to share that faith with others. But how does this faith affect the goals that we set for the church? It leads to optimism.

In the tiny church, there is danger in two extremes. One extreme is in the elimination of faith in the goal-setting or planning process. This happens when the people of the church have a low perception of themselves. Lyle Schaller says,

> When our perception of reality falls below what really is . . . we will tend to make modest plans . . . The lower our self-esteem, the more likely it is that we will concentrate on our problems and on institutional survival rather than on the potentialities for ministry.[3]

It is possible for faith to be eliminated or given little place, forgetting that the God who empowered the Early Church on the Day of Pentecost can be trusted to empower them and make them effective in their corner of the world. Their focus tends to be on what they see in themselves, rather than on the God in whom they trust who has gifted them to serve where they are. What must be kept in mind is that God lavishes His grace—His spiritual gifts—upon all Christians, in big churches, small churches, and tiny churches. If we believe that, it is strategic that we discover those gifts. Regardless of how a church views itself, those gifts are there! The church will do a better job in setting helpful goals for the fulfillment of its Christ-directed mission if there is optimistic, honest acknowledgment of their present strengths. Such a godly self-appraisal can lead to optimistic expectancy.

In his book titled *Twelve Keys to an Effective Church*, Kennon L. Callahan states:

> Realistically knowing and strongly affirming those strengths that the church has going for it is decisive for success. Substantial power is generated as a congregation discovers and claims its strengths: Power for the

future is found in claiming our strengths, not in focusing on our weaknesses and shortcomings.[4]

It may be concluded that strengths are developed by people empowered by God through the Holy Spirit. To deny this, even in the place where nothing seems to be happening, is to deny God. Finding and claiming them is to claim for the church the compelling presence of God in His power. By setting goals that are optimistic because they reflect these strengths from God, the church becomes poised to accomplish His purposes in their midst and in their area of responsibility.

Attainable Goals

Goals must be **attainable.** Because Christians are persons of faith in the Almighty God, they believe that "nothing is impossible with Him" (Luke 1:37), and of course that is a correct declaration of faith. Their zeal, however, may cause the tiny church to set excessive and unrealistic goals. The hearts of these well-meaning persons are certainly in the right place, and they are sincere in what they suggest. But we must ask, "How would the people of a church of 20 members feel if they set a goal for 100 members in a year, and they ended up with 50?" That is superb growth, yet many may see themselves as failures because they missed their goal. Failure to set realistic, attainable goals may actually lead to discouragement and disappointment. Those who worked so hard may be prone to frustration, and the end result may have a negative impact upon the long-term growth of the congregation.[5]

On the other hand, goals should require more than average effort. Goals should cause us to stretch. There must be a healthy balance between faith and challenge on the one hand, and realism and attainability on the other. Goals based on hopes, desires, and wishes alone are not usually very realistic. Goals that combine faith with reality will help the tiny church to realize some victories in their ministries, leading to a greater sense of vision, optimism, and expectancy.

Lay-Developed Goals

The tiny church must be reminded that lay involvement develops a sense of ownership that is strategic. Seeing the church as "our church" will help laypersons take responsibility for its operation. If this is true, then it is important for these people to have a sense of ownership concerning the goals and purpose of the church. This is far better than asking them to rubber-stamp imposed goals. Possibilities are born when they help author goals toward the fulfillment of a purpose. A vision is planted that opens the door for thought and initiative, resulting in fruitful ministry.

Specific Goals

Two dangers to avoid in setting specific goals are these: not listing any goals at all, and making them so complicated they are hard to understand. On the one hand, it may not be necessarily that the church has set *no* goals, but that they have not written them down for proper reflection or clarification. This leads to a vague sense of what the church is to do specifically to fulfill its purpose.

The other extreme is in making the goals too complicated. Goals need to be specific, clarifying what purpose statements describe in general terms. Specific, measurable goals help a church see for themselves their progress. When they look back and ask, "Was the goal achieved?" there is a measurable standard for self-evaluation. Success, in turn, provides its own motivation to work toward the accomplishment of new goals.

It has been stated that "most small churches lack that kind of clarity in their statements of church goals. Yet they have deep commitments to the purposes of the church."[6] If this is true, perhaps one can state that commitment is not usually the hindrance to effectiveness—clarity is. Specific goals enrich understanding and provide a tool for measuring progress. Sensing that accomplishment has been made in the name of Christ, the people's faith is increased, motivating them to new conquest.

Don't Set Them and Then Forget Them

As important as goals may be, they are only helpful if there is a person or a group of persons to implement and monitor them. Unused goals are worthless. They must be taken from the writing pad and put into action. Though it is ultimately the pastor's responsibility to see that progress is realized and recognized, there is also a need to appoint a person or persons to be responsible for monitoring the goals, allocating resources, and instituting programs to fulfill the goals.

To carelessly set out to list goals without a sense of diligence, thoughtfulness, and faith will do more harm than good. There are risks for the tiny church in setting goals, and traps that may actually hamper the desired progress. The potential benefits, however, make it worth attempting. Whatever the setting and size of the church, the same truth applies: God has called His people to be His representatives to touch their corner of the world. It may be an area of declining neighborhoods or of a depressed economy. Or the church may be surrounded by larger, stronger churches. But God has given them a unique purpose, and His grace and power will enable them to do His will.

So set goals that are helpful, and then begin to work, trust, and expect. The goals are not ends in themselves, but they will point to what God has done—through you and your church.

Set realistic goals.

4

In Order to Be Fishers, We Must Fish

The following parable was quoted in the book *The Master's Plan for Making Disciples:*

Now it came to pass that a group existed who called themselves fishermen. And lo, there were many fish in the waters all around. In fact, the whole area was surrounded by streams and lakes filled with fish. And the fish were hungry.

Week after week, month after month, and year after year these, who called themselves fishermen, met in meetings and talked about their call to go about fishing.

Continually they searched for new and better methods of fishing and for new and better definitions of fishing. They sponsored costly nationwide and worldwide congresses to discuss fishing and to promote fishing and hear about all the ways of fishing, such as the new fishing equipment, fish calls, and whether any new bait was discovered.

These fishermen built large, beautiful buildings called "Fishing Headquarters." The plea was that everyone should be a fisherman and every fisherman should fish. One thing they didn't do, however; they didn't fish.

All the fishermen seemed to agree that what is needed is a board which could challenge fishermen to be faithful in fishing. The board was formed by those who had the great vision and courage to speak about fishing, to define fishing, and to promote the idea of fishing in far-away streams and lakes where many other fish of different colors lived.

Large, elaborate, and expensive training centers were built whose purpose was to teach fishermen how to fish. Those who taught had doctorates in fishology. But the teachers did not fish. They only taught fishing.

Some spent much study and travel to learn the history of fishing and to see far-away places where the founding fathers did great fishing in the centuries past. They lauded the faithful fishermen of years before who handed down the idea of fishing.

Many who felt the call to be fishermen responded. They were commissioned and sent to fish. And they went off to foreign lands . . . to teach fishing.

Now it's true that many of the fishermen sacrificed and put up with all kinds of difficulties. Some lived near the water and bore the smell of dead fish every day. They received the ridicule of some who made fun of their fishermen's clubs. They anguished over those who were not committed enough to attend the weekly meetings to talk about fishing. After all, were they not following the Master who said, "Follow me, and I will make you fishers of men"?

Imagine how hurt some were when one day a person suggested that those who don't catch fish were really not fishermen, no matter how much they claimed to be. Yet it did sound correct. Is a person a fisherman if year after year he/she never catches a fish? Is one following if he/she isn't fishing?[1]

The Great Commission of Jesus Christ to the Church is that we personally take His gospel to the people of the world. It has been read and pondered by individuals in large churches and tiny churches alike, and it is very true that a church that neglects the evangelization of the world and its community is not very Christian. Evangelism is essential if the church is indeed to be the Church of Jesus Christ.

Kinds of Growth

For most tiny churches, evangelism will be the *only*

means of real growth. There are three basic kinds of growth in the church. **Biological growth** happens because children are born into the church and eventually accept Christ as Lord and Savior. Then their children accept Christ. This is a good form of growth—families coming into the experience of salvation in response to the good news of Jesus Christ. But for most churches, especially tiny ones, biological growth is unreliable at best. In our society, children grow up and move away. Most will not be around that particular church when they have families. As important as this kind of growth is, it must be stated that the church cannot depend upon it for a sustained growth pattern.

In a second kind of growth, **transfer growth,** one church increases at the expense of others. There may be transfer members from churches in the area or from out-of-town churches as persons move and relocate their families. What must be realized is that, in most cases, transfer growth will not be very significant. Most churches will transfer out approximately the same number of members as transfer in. Such is usually not the case with the tiny church. If the tiny church is in a rural setting, as so many are, there simply is little movement of people from the urban or suburban setting to the rural environment. Thus, transfer growth is more likely to be transfer decline.

If the tiny church is in a suburban setting, there are still reasons for not depending upon the transfer of members for growth. The most common is that persons who transfer into the suburbs tend generally to seek out a larger church. Those who have served or attended a tiny church in such a setting will understand this trend. That is not a criticism; it is a fact of life. Even in the suburban setting, the tiny church will lose more members by transfer than it will receive. Since this is the case, the tiny church must not depend upon transfer growth, even in areas where population growth is significant.

The third kind of growth is **conversion growth,** or

growth through evangelism. This is the one way the tiny church can be effective, fruitful, and growing. In all honesty, this is the only true form of growth for the church. Paul R. Orjala writes,

> The truth is that there is not real church growth until someone is saved. Accessions by transfer are important for the individuals involved, but it is like taking money out of one pocket and putting it in another—it doesn't mean that there is no money. Evangelism is at the center of church growth.[2]

Sustained growth, therefore, comes through conversion growth—reaching the lost of the community with the gospel of Jesus Christ. Evangelism is the major contributor of growth, if not the only long-term contributor for the tiny church.

There are circumstances that may hinder statistical growth—an exodus of members to other states, a contentious past, oppressive financial indebtedness, to name a few. Growth may come more slowly in some places than others, and often not until troubling issues are resolved. Or, it may be that the church has been doing a good job of evangelizing the lost, only to see them move away. The lack of growth for a church does not mean that it is failing any more than great growth always means success. The principle is very clear:

YOU CAN EVANGELIZE WITHOUT GROWTH, BUT THERE IS NOT GROWTH WITHOUT EVANGELISM.

Perspective of the Church

What, then, must the tiny church deal with that is uniquely a part of its setting? There are four issues that the tiny church must examine. The first is **perspective.** Perhaps it would be well for its people to ask the question, "Are we satisfied with our church as it exists today?" When the church is viewed as one basic, caring cell, the answer is neither complicated nor judgmental.

The tiny church is already the right size for everyone to know everybody else, or at least to know about them. One of the essential characteristics of the small or tiny church is the "capacity to care about people personally."[3] The perspective of the church makes a difference. Growth can be seen as either a disruption to such intimacy, or as the exciting result of sharing care and love with others outside of the church fellowship. How a church views its fellowship in relation to others will make a difference.

Purpose of the Church

Again we are brought to the issue of **purpose** in the church. What are we here for? What are we supposed to be and do? Coupled with purpose must be the willingness to change—for the sake of the church's mission. If there is the sincere desire to penetrate the community for Christ, then the possibilities are unlimited. A motivation to confront lovingly those persons in the community who are lost with the wondrous truths and liberating grace of the gospel of Jesus Christ will ensure substantial ministry and possible growth. The key is not only what the church desires to do, but how much it gives of itself in the name of the Lord, using the tools available for ministry. When evangelism is the central focus of the church, there are opportunities for miracles.

Priorities of the Church

What the church determines as its **priorities** will make a difference in terms of growth and evangelism. For instance, some churches may opt to stay in a declining neighborhood rather than relocate in a growing suburb. Such a decision may result in less growth but greater faithfulness. Another priority factor is the proportion of the pastor's time and energy spent on the members and personal concerns of the congregation. What proportion of time is spent on developing and implementing ministries for outreach and evangelism? In most tiny churches, the pastor spends a good proportion of time in maintenance activities—lawn mowing and trimming, church cleaning, building maintenance—that deter from activities that foster growth. He also spends a good proportion of time in people maintenance. Lyle Schaller states that the pastor is "the key factor" in any strategy for outreach, and that this

> usually means that a large proportion of the minister's time and energy must be reserved for face-to-face contacts with potential new members and new members. Obviously that reduces the amount of time the minister has to spend with [the established] members. This is one of the basic prices of church growth, and one that many members are unwilling to pay.[4]

The priorities the tiny church sets for itself will make a significant difference in its potential for evangelism and growth.

Product of the Church

The fourth consideration is their **product.** Ultimately, growth is not the final product for the church—sharing the love and grace of God through Jesus Christ is. Jon Johnston states, "The primary task of the church, be it small or large, is NOT merely to produce people to fill empty pews. Rather, it is to offer everyone the love of God in the name of Jesus."[5] If that is not our product, then consumers will not "buy" it. May we present to our Lord new and growing disciples that please Him and bring Him honor, glory, and praise!

Personal Passion of the Church

Evangelism is the mission that Christ has given to His Church and to each Christian. As surely as we acknowledge the need and responsibility for evangelism, we must personally set out to do it. Our Lord did not instruct us to appoint a select few to be an evangelism committee and leave the work to them. He does not expect us to give only token effort. Rather, the call is for each of us, not only to get our hands dirty with the bait of fishing, but to bring in the fish—to be active in bringing others to a personal relationship with Him. This cannot be done by hiding behind a desk or by confinement in a church building. The call is for every Christian to be a fisher of men—and that means you and me. No excuses!

Jesus compared His small group of followers to a "little flock" (Luke 12:32). Other passages, such as John 10, describe our relationship with Christ in terms of sheep and their shepherd. The only way to get more sheep is for the sheep to reproduce. The Church grows only as it reproduces disciples. Jesus said to Peter and Andrew, "Come, follow me, . . . and I will make you fishers of men" (Matt. 4:19). Jesus' message is very distinct—the Church must grow; it must evangelize the world. To catch fish, there must be fishers.

In order to be fishers, we must fish.

5

The Body Is...
Made Up of Many Parts

The apostle Paul's instruction to the churches in 1 Corinthians 12 is addressed to the "body of Christ" (v. 27). He was writing to a problem church—a church that was self-defeating. Paul exhorts them to be united together in Christ and to work together just as the parts of the body work together. Examine the following three verses:

Verse 12—"The body is a unit, though it is made up of many parts; and though all its parts are many, they form one body. So it is with Christ."

Verse 14—"Now the body is not made up of one part but of many."

Verse 20—"As it is, there are many parts, but one body."

In speaking of "many parts," Paul makes clear that the Body of Christ, the Church, is not the responsibility of one individual or member. It is comprised of persons who join themselves together in a common faith and a common purpose for a united pursuit. Such cannot be the case if a Christian attempts to live for Christ and serve Him apart from the rest of the Body.

Eph. 4:1-16 also speaks directly to this point:

Verse 16—"From him [Christ] the whole body, joined and held together by every supporting ligament, grows and builds itself up in love, as each part does its work."

This verse implies that the body has multiple parts. It metaphorically describes the Church of Jesus Christ not as an institution but as an organism. The organism functions when its members work together for that which has brought them together. The message is clear—the Body of Christ must have parts, or members, if it is to carry out its intended purpose.

Because of fewer members, the tiny church may not have as wide a diversity of abilities. Is it possible to be a body of Christ with not many parts? This is a critical question for the tiny church. Another way of asking it is "How few is too few?" How many persons does a church need to be a viable Body of Christ, meeting one another's needs?

The principle of critical mass, or the minimum number of persons or resources needed to accomplish a specific task, is not new. A business, to compete, must have a certain amount of capital and man-hours. A scientist must be provided a properly equipped laboratory and assistants to accomplish research. An athletic team must have enough players to fill every position. Even our human bodies need a certain amount of essential nutrients for us to live and function in a healthy manner. Critical mass is a common principle in the many facets of daily life.

The problem of critical mass must be confronted by the tiny church. Carl Dudley describes this problem in the small or tiny church:

> There is a "critical mass" of assembled people necessary for a program to feel "right" to the participants. There may not be enough women available for an association, or youth for a communicants class, or toddlers for a church-hour nursery.[1]

This raises the question, "How tiny may a church be and still be effective as the continuation of the earthly ministry of Jesus Christ?" It is difficult and perhaps unwise to define critical mass in terms of numbers of people. There are too many factors influencing a church's viability.

The distinction will be handled differently by a "church-type mission" than by an organized church. In the church-type mission, there must be a sufficient number of committed people who will give their allegiance to the fellowship and its ultimate reason for organizing. If there is not a sufficient group to form the critical mass, evidence would suggest that inadequate resources preclude the formation of a full-scale church ministry at that time.

The tiny church, already officially organized, does not have the opportunity to make such an evaluation. If there are not sufficient resources to carry out effective ministry, they must take another approach to critical mass to accomplish their goals. Instead of focusing upon what they do not have, perhaps it would be better to take what is available and simply use it for the honor and glory of God. A tiny church can use its potential as servants of God by:

T Thanking God for each other
A Assessing the possibilities
K Kindling a burning passion for ministry
E Expecting God to bless their efforts for Him

Thank God for Each Other

First of all, begin by **thanking God for each other.** Sometimes we become so discouraged by the people and resources we don't have that we forget about those that God has given us. He knows what we need, and we can trust Him for that. Perhaps if we thank Him for the Christian brothers and sisters He has given to us, He will use us to bring others into that Christian family. If we fall into the godly habit of thanking God for each other, the natural response is to love and care for others outside the church fellowship a little more too. So thank God for what He has already given you—each other.

Assess the Possibilities

Once we begin to thank God for each other rather than bemoaning our weaknesses, we will begin to see the possibilities that have been hidden to the church as a whole. It will become apparent that each person really *is* gifted in one way or another. There will be the realization that God has given different persons "grace-enhanced abilities" to do some things well for God. Slowly the covers of ingrown opinions and limitation will be removed by the winds of possibilities within that tiny church. When those possibilities are assessed, members will discover that God has empowered them so that they might be effective in carrying out His mission.

Kindle a Burning Passion for Ministry

This leads naturally to the third step—**kindle a burning passion for ministry.** Once the tiny church has discovered that, regardless of their size or even their weaknesses, they have been given by Almighty God grace and possibilities for ministry, they must envision what they will do, and then set out to do it. It is good to thank God for each other and even to assess the possibilities, but the best of possibilities never become more than that until they are translated into overt action. Between the assessing and the possessing comes the doing. Until the tiny church honors the Lord by ministering to others in His name, the best will never be realized. A passion for ministry will make a difference in its sphere of influence.

Expect God to Bless Your Efforts for Him

Sometimes we do not live out what we say we believe. We say we have faith in God, but we don't really expect Him to work through us or bless our efforts for Him. A good promise to claim is the one found in Hab. 1:5—"Look . . . and be utterly amazed. For I am going to do something in your days that you would not believe, even if you were told."

Some churches have gone too long in *not* expecting God to bless their efforts for Him, and it is time to anticipate God's double blessing just to make up for lost time! God is not stingy! He wants to enable and empower those who, in faithfulness and obedience, set out to make a difference in their communities. God is waiting for His people to reach out a loving hand to those around them who need His salvation. When the tiny church focuses on their call to ministry, God will take what they give to Him—money, time, energy—and will multiply it for His glory and honor. Indeed, regardless of how sufficient or insufficient your church's critical mass might be, you can expect God to bless your efforts for Him when you use what He has given you. When you think about it, that is really all He asks of us, isn't it?

So how few is too few? Maybe those of us who are part of a tiny church should concentrate on a different question: "What does God desire of *us*?" Our omniscient God knows how tiny or large we are—how weak or strong we are. He does not concern himself with what a church *does not* have, but what it *does* have and what it does with that. As important as critical mass may be, it is not the final, determining factor. For who would have thought that a poor, helpless baby in a manger in a Bethlehem stable would so change the world? Even the Sanhedrin did not think the "ignorant" disciples of Jesus could do anything they should fear. Yet look what God did through the likes of Peter and his fisher friends. The Lord's grace and power are no less for you in your tiny church!

The Body is . . . made up of many parts.

6

Do a Few Things, and Do Them Well

The shopping mall has become a popular attraction for both old and young. When you think about it, there are several good reasons for this. The shopping mall is enclosed; thus, the climate remains the same—no rain or snow, no extreme heat or cold. One can shop or jog or just look around with no concern for the weather. But there is another good reason for the popularity of the shopping mall.

Unlike the large, independently owned department stores of yesteryears, the shopping mall of today claims from two to five or more such stores. In addition, a shopping mall would be incomplete without the dozens of small, specialty shops—shops for jeans and tuxedos, for shoes and boots, for electronics and office supplies, for jewelry and greeting cards. These stores are tiny compared to their giant, department-store neighbors.

It would be foolish for the small shops to try to compete with their larger neighbors. They are limited by resources and space, but they have found a place in the marketplace of our nation. By limiting their inventories and specializing, they do what they can do best. And they often do it better than the general merchandisers.

Perhaps the tiny church can learn from this principle. The church in general is a bit like a shopping mall. Like the department stores, the larger churches seem to attract most of the people. They offer the most to those who pass through their doors. They are the ones most people hear about in news and advertising. But like the shops, the many small and tiny churches are an integral part of the total church picture. As the shopping mall would be incomplete without its variety, the Church today would be incomplete without the tiny, the small, and the large churches. It is better equipped to take the gospel to the world through its kaleidoscope of churches of varying size and character.

The tiny church must resist the temptation to copy their larger neighbors. It is unnecessary to have a choir simply because the church down the block has one, or to strive for a dynamic youth ministry like First Church's, unless its strengths lie in those areas. Large churches often have programs every night of the week, offering something for everyone. The temptation for the tiny church is to try to cover all the bases and fill the weekly and monthly calendars with activity. That is often destructive, for the tiny church's product is not as expansive as the "major department store" kind of church. Instead, the tiny church needs to recognize its specialty status and make it the best on the market.

A major problem within the tiny church is that of spreading itself thin in terms of effective ministry. The basic organizational and ministry expectations of the denomination would more than deplete the total resources of the tiny church. It may be extremely difficult to staff a fully graded Sunday School with ministries for children, youth, and adults, world missions programs, denominational emphases, et al., if less than a dozen persons are involved in ministry. Kennon Callahan addresses this point as it relates to the church in general:

> It is regrettable that local congregations consume so much of an individual's time in committee meetings that they have very little time left over to participate in their church's mission in the world. Effective congregations conserve their members' time by developing the most minimal and streamlined organizational structure

possible, so that people can be involved substantively and responsibly in the total life and mission of the church.[1]

To attempt to do everything a church seemingly is expected to do may actually be more of a hindrance than a help. If the church spends so much time and energy in organizational and traditional ministries that their mission and purpose is neglected, they will be less effective in ministering to their community.

Along with the difficulties of inadequate resources comes the problem of burnout. Frustration and overwork besiege members of the tiny church who are forced to function in several capacities when a variety of ministries are undertaken. Frustration builds because they feel they cannot give their best to any of these tasks. Then the dilemma is "Should I resign this job for that one?" when there is no replacement for either position. Add to this the realization that the church is not growing even with their hard and faithful work, and the result is discouragement, guilt, and a loss of vision. There is no time for outreach after the traditional ministries are carried out. The problem is real and must be addressed, for the results defeat the very purpose of the tiny church.

What, then, must they do? How can they be effective while existing in the shadow of the larger church? They must be specialists, adhering to a simple principle: **Do a few things, and do them well.** Three basic considerations can help the tiny church do that: **strengths, structure,** and **stress.**

The Strengths of the Tiny Church

The first consideration the tiny church must make in determining its ministry has to do with its strengths. In what areas is the church strong? What do they do best? A good place to begin their self-examination is with spiritual gifts of the church's members. They should be encouraged to:

45

1. Explore the possibilities.
2. Experiment with as many as possible.
3. Examine their true feelings.
4. Evaluate their effectiveness.
5. Expect confirmation from the body.[2]

The apostle Paul writes about spiritual gifts in 1 Cor. 12: 4-7: "There are different kinds of gifts, but the same Spirit. There are different kinds of service, but the same Lord. There are different kinds of working, but the same God works all of them in all men. Now to each one the manifestation of the Spirit is given for the common good." If we believe this is true, then *every* church has its strengths, even the tiny ones! The key is in openly and honestly seeking to find how God has uniquely equipped His Body of Christ to carry on the ministry begun by Jesus. It has been stated that "growing churches specialize in what works best for them."[3] Perhaps such a statement is true because such churches have identified their strengths—how God has empowered them for effective ministry in His name. When the tiny church does this, they can then develop ministries that utilize their strengths.

The Structure of the Tiny Church

The structure of the tiny church pertains to the method and organization it employs to carry out what it can do best. It has been suggested that Mark 2:27 could be paraphrased, "The structure should serve the church, not the church the structure."[4] Suggested organizational requirements and structure may be applicable for some traditional ministries, but what is most important is that the structure provide the impetus and support for ministry in the particular setting. In most cases, the organizational structure that works in large, and even in small, churches is too cumbersome for what the tiny church is striving to accomplish. Complexity and management flow charts would be superfluous. It is unnecessary to assign church board members to six or seven committees when there are only seven persons on the board! A good rule to live by is this: keep it simple! A simple, basic structure will serve the tiny church well.

The Stress of the Tiny Church

The third consideration has to do with stress. What will our ministry emphasis be? Will we try to do everything we can as a church, or will we focus our efforts in areas where God has particularly enabled us? The stress of ministry will fall in one of two practices: "Do a little bit of everything" or "Do a little and do it well." To focus on the former may not be entirely wrong, for the church would probably be sincere in its efforts to provide ministry for everyone. But to focus on doing a little of everything ignores the God-given gifts and abilities present for effective ministry.

It is true that focusing on strengths will limit the activities of the church to some degree. The transmission of the gospel, however, is accomplished more effectively when God's people minister as they are enabled, rather than ministering in ways for which they are not suited because they are expected to do so. Methodology is not as important as the message. When our stress is funneled into quality ministry that meets the needs of people, growth and effectiveness will occur spontaneously.

One of the assets in so many tiny churches is the determination of the members. Few organizations would attempt to sustain the kinds and numbers of activity with as few people as the tiny church often does. But their commitment to God and to His Church undergird their resolve. What is needed is not the dismantling of that committed effort and determination, but the directing of it in positive, effective, unified ways.

Once again we point to specialization as the solution to lack of ministry personnel and other resources. The tiny church has possibilities that can become opportunities for ministry when it does what it does best. If its few members possessed no good qualities or strengths, it probably would not exist at all! So find those strengths, acknowledge them, and direct available resources toward ministry that uses them.

Do a few things, and do them well.

7

If We're in It Together, Let's Do It Together

Throughout the New Testament, the Christian life is described within the context of the Christian community, meeting the needs of people. The Christian does not live an isolated existence; rather, he lives out his faith with others as together they grow and mature in Christlikeness.

One passage of Scripture that highlights this community concept is 1 Pet. 2:9: "But you are a chosen people, a royal priesthood, a holy nation, a people belonging to God." As stated in an earlier chapter, the church consists of a diversity of individuals who come together and commit themselves to one another. God accomplishes His design for His Church through us as we come together and meet one another's needs. Reuben Welch said it well: "We really do need each other!"

In many ways, churches are like people. This is not at all surprising, since churches are comprised of people. By joining together to form associations and parachurch organizations, churches have learned they can accomplish what none of them could do alone. A good example would be local churches uniting within a denomination to establish a downtown mission where the poor are fed, clothed, and helped spiritually.

However, these joint efforts are directed toward a select group of people or projects. A district, for instance, collects funds from the various churches to sponsor home mission works, ethnic ministries, and other missionary enterprises of the church. District ministries such as youth camps and retreats, children's camps, and retreats for laypersons are also important as churches on the district work together in selected ways. Few, if any of these churches could accomplish these significant ministries and projects singly.

What is rather peculiar is that some churches will not cooperate in ministry with a sister church that is nearby. It may not be a conscious lack of concern or cooperation, but the tendency is, for one reason or another, for churches that are geographically close to each other to become separated, even though they carry the same denominational label. These churches miss the opportunity to make a joint impact on their locale.

In larger churches, this particular concern may not be something to keep their leaders awake at night, for they already have a good variety of ministries and activities for their people and their community. However, the tiny church with its limited resources cannot provide everything it wants and needs for the people of its fellowship, even though it is able to make a positive difference in their lives. Some needs will be left unfulfilled. When such a tiny church exists near one or more larger churches of the same denomination, the problem is obviously magnified for them.

The cooperation of two or more churches, preferably of the same denomination, can enhance overall ministry for the smaller church as well as for the large churches. The principle that states, "If we're in it together, let's work together," allows for greater need meeting through sharing.

Cooperation between churches near one another would, on a small scale, apply the principles that bring churches together as districts. The concept of cooperative ministry is not a new one, but fear of competition often hinders such a process. Competition should never exist between churches. A cooperative spirit, however, may be a tangible way of sharing the love of Christ.

The question that must be asked, then, is this: "What are some realistic ways that cooperation may assist the tiny church in fulfilling the Great Commission of Christ?" The options are as endless as your creativity. Several possibilities immediately come to mind. Extended ministry—in which the larger church shares with the tiny church in revivals, concerts, and special services—Vacation Bible School and other special children's ministries, as well as seminars and workshops are good examples. There are numerous opportunities for the larger church to share with its tiny neighbor. Such sharing provides the people of the tiny church the chance to be involved in special, helpful events that they could not provide on their own.

Professional staffing for the tiny church can be offered through circuitry. Many denominations have used the concept of the "circuit" to staff their smallest churches. In the circuit, two or more churches are served by one pastor. There are advantages and disadvantages with such an arrangement, but it offers some possibilities for the tiny church that does not have sufficient income to provide staffing.

Another possibility is for the larger sister church and the tiny church to hire the same person. This individual could serve the tiny church as pastor and the larger church as a part-time associate pastor. In certain settings, such an agreement could be helpful to both churches.

A third form of cooperation is called "group ministry." In group ministry, two or more churches join forces to work together in certain programs. The options would be determined by the settings, whether in youth ministry, a singles' group, or missions rallies, but the potential exists for exciting ministry. What is important is not that activity be created, but that meaningful, effective ministry be accomplished that helps each church fulfill its purpose.

If cooperative ministry is to be successful, several potential problems must be avoided. One problem is that churches often cooperate out of weakness. As Lyle Schaller states,

> Too often, cooperative ministries are launched out of a sense of frustration, powerlessness, fear, or hopelessness and are assigned responsibilities that have proved impossible for the congregations to respond to unilaterally or that are too explosive for any one congregation to cope with by itself. Placing these duds and bombs at the top of the agenda of the cooperative ministry is one means of accentuating the fragility of intercongregational cooperation.[1]

The tendency is to work together in an endeavor where none of the churches has been successful. To put together the weaknesses of a group of churches will still yield weak results.

Another problem may arise with the misconception that cooperation and growth are "incompatible." Schaller indicates that this is "an example of a trade-off."[2] What often happens is that the small or tiny church either chooses to involve itself in a cooperative venture with one or more churches, or it pursues an aggressive recruitment or evangelistic effort. Unfortunately, few churches do both. For some reason, people who have a strong interest in evangelism and church growth are not usually interested in cooperative church efforts, and those who are interested in cooperative projects usually are interested for other reasons. However, there is a danger that the tiny church could expend so much effort in working in cooperative ministry that time and resources are depleted for effective outreach and evangelism.

A third consideration for the tiny church in cooperative ministry is that of identity—a particular quality that allows it to carry on a unique and exclusive ministry in its setting. In a cooperative ministry this identity may become blurred or overshadowed by the larger church partner. People unite with a specific church, not because of cooperative ministries, but because of its distinctives as a worshiping and ministering group of believers. Such a positive and attracting identity must be preserved.

These problems need not be an argument against cooperative ministry, but potential difficulties need to be addressed. The church then has a greater opportunity to discover its best options for ministry.

Three basic suggestions may help the tiny church to approach their options wisely:

1. **Be selective.**
2. **Share strengths.**
3. **Look for supplemental ministries.**

Selectivity in your cooperative projects will help preserve your distinctive identity. Nothing will erode that more quickly than overkill. In fact, no matter how tiny the church may be, it will not need everything the larger church or churches are offering. Your church must not depend upon others for the strengths it already possesses, but it should choose to work with other churches in ways that will help itself as well as them.

Second, **share your strengths.** What does your church do well? Sharing strengths will provide quality ministry. But be wise enough to share, not deplete. Make sure that your tiny church's mission is not compromised. Remember the principle, "Do a few things, and do them well."

Third, **look for supplemental ministries.** Keep your eyes open for new, creative ways to minister together in the name of the Lord. What is the larger church planning that could be helpful to your tiny church? The larger church may take some things for granted and not think about inviting the people of your church to participate, so the pastor or leaders of the tiny church must be alert to such possibilities and be willing to ask. Look for ministries that supplement what your church is already doing.

Sometimes neighboring churches are in competition with one another, though that would never be admitted. The impression is made, "You work in your area, and we work in ours." But each church should exist for the same reason—to make disciples of the people in their communities, to spread the good news of Jesus Christ to all the world. If that is the case, they can work together without fear of losing members to each other and without competition. "If we're in it together, let's work together."

8

Finance Is More than Paying the Bills

It would be naive to believe that, because the church is concerned with spiritual matters, finances for fellowship and ministry will always be there. Many tiny churches face difficult financial decisions as they sometimes struggle to continue their ministries to congregation and community.

Every congregation must meet basic financial obligations—a pastor's salary, a meeting place, maintenance, utilities, and miscellaneous supplies. Because of their limited financial base, the people of the tiny church expend most of their energies keeping the institution alive and financially solvent.[1] The reality of the situation is that

> there is an irreducible minimum budget for all churches, whether they are large or small. If they attempt to maintain an adequate building for worship, education, and community gatherings, plus a paid ministry, a basic budget will be required regardless of size of membership.[2]

The tiny church must come to grips with the fact of basic, budgetary needs if it is to be the effective, vital church it desires to be. But there is more to finance than just paying the bills. Church leaders must make wise, careful, thoughtful decisions. It is not that money is the most important consideration of the church, but that unwise financial decisions can cripple the tiny church. Five considerations are of immense importance:

Finances and Priorities

Limited funds must be disbursed on priorities established by the church's leaders. Perceived needs of the church in fulfilling its purpose are of primary importance. At the same time, care must be taken that decisions today will not hamper the church in future years or set financial policies that restrict future leaders.

The church must determine real issues and remember that "money is *not* the issue in faithfulness and effectiveness." The real issues for the church are:

1. Are the perceived needs necessities, options, or luxuries?
2. Is the church funding maintenance for the sake of survival, or for ministry and mission needs?
3. Will the bottom-line figure be a snap, a challenge, or an oppressive burden?
4. Is the pastor being fairly compensated for expected time and abilities?
5. How will the church raise the funds to underwrite its perceived need?
6. Will the necessary income be given by a broad base of supporters, or a disproportionate few?[3]

The church is responsible to disburse funds wisely in ways that lead to effective outreach and ministry. In determining priorities, the tiny church should seek to be free from financial concerns that detract from its central reason for existence.

Finances and Pastoral Staffing

Because of financial limitations, the tiny church might consider staffing options other than the traditional full-time pastor. Since less time is needed to minister to the members and needs of the congregation, pastoral duties could be fulfilled by a part-time person. Or consider a lay pastor. Many church missions or new churches have been led by a competent layperson, with the only financial obligation being reimbursement for travel expense. Other possibilities include, as noted earlier, the circuit concept or the large church sharing an associate pastor with the tiny church. Another option is a bivocational pastor, who is secularly employed. In some settings, these options would not be possible at all; in others, they could work only if volunteers from the congregation would assume the time-consuming duties that often fall to the pastor of a small church such as mowing the church lawn, painting, maintenance, and custodial work.

Possibilities are available to the tiny church that will be creative and open to new ideas.

Finances and Subsidy

Perhaps one of the most crucial financial considerations for the tiny church has to do with **finances and subsidy.** The question is this: If the tiny church does not have sufficient financial resources to meet perceived needs, should another church or the district financially subsidize that church? This question has been extensively debated in the last two decades and presents problems that the tiny church and its district leaders would need to examine. The bottom line is that all churches must, over the long term, be self-supporting. How this can be accomplished and what is best for the tiny church will need to be hammered out. Other issues and expectations are secondary.

Many church growth experts have concluded that financial subsidy has a negative impact on a church. Carl Dudley says, "The largest number and the heartiest of small churches are in those denominations where funds [for subsidizing] are simply not available."[4] One study concludes that "the introduction of denominational procedures, including financial support, seemed to reduce the resolve of the congregation to retain its independence."[5] What may happen is that, in its attempt to help the financially needy church, the district creates new problems, not the least of which is the problem of dependence. Jack Radford, in *Planting New Churches,* states that

> documented research can be provided to show that mission congregations can become too dependent, much like children who have been given too much by overly benevolent parents. Such dependency inhibits growth and stable development of the new congregation. A welfare syndrome can develop quicker than can a responsible attitude where finances are concerned.[6]

Subsidizing tends to deplete faith in a church when the people relax and depend on the district rather than on God. In addition, it is believed that the church's morale suffers because it is not able to "pay its own way." Lyle Schaller states conclusively and emphatically, "Financial subsidies and high morale rarely go together!"[7] The tiny church and the district must be aware of these negative concerns in discussing possible financial partnership.

On the other hand, there are those who contend that financial subsidy may help the tiny church, if handled appropriately. Such help can be crucial in the initial stages of a church's life as stated by Ezra Earl Jones: "Where inadequate initial support results in weak congregations, the future extension of the church and sharing of the gospel is sacrificed." In fact, Jones suggests that no new church should be organized unless the denomination is prepared to subsidize that congregation with a minimum of $90,000 to $150,000 during its first five years (1976 dollar amounts).[8]

Those who understand the value of financial subsidy also perceive the potential problems as summarized above, but these individuals believe that new, needy churches should not be allowed to starve. The new congregation should not, they contend, be "pushed so hard that it becomes incapacitated and overly concerned with finances during its first initial years."[9] The new church needs flexibility and freedom from financial pressures as it strives to establish itself as a vital, viable congregation.

In our day of high building costs, there are several principles that a tiny church, its district, and its denomination must consider as they examine the possibility of financial subsidy or options to traditional forms of subsidy. If the church should receive help, five principles should be involved:

1. **Agree in advance to limits for subsidy.** Set limits that will avoid dependency and enhance self-respect. Whether such subsidy comes from a larger church or the district, author a plan that will phase out the financial support, preferably over a period of five years or less.

2. **Determine and define the purpose of the subsidy.** Is the subsidy to provide assistance in planting a new church? To prolong the life of the church? Or is the subsidy to support a vital ministry that needs some short-term help? In any case, it should strengthen the tiny church, not perpetuate weakness.

3. **Consider a "lump sum" subsidy payment in initial days of the new church.** Because of the high costs involved in planting a new church, providing a parsonage, purchasing land, and constructing a permanent facility, consider some district provision so that the new church will not be burdened with excessive indebtedness.

4. **Consider a "phase-in" plan for denominational budget allotments.** A new business usually does not provide dividends for its investors in the initial few years. Similarly, the new church could be allowed the opportunity to gradually assume responsibility for important denominational needs. To be hit with them all at once makes self-support harder to reach.

5. **Consider the unique characteristics of the tiny church when denominational budgets are allotted.** If it is true that all churches, regardless of size, have an irreducible minimum budget, then the amount set should allow even the smallest church to function and meet its own needs. *That* amount should be used as an exemption from the total used in determining these allotments (i.e., subtracted from the budget base), not simply a "token" amount such as $3,000. In fact, even the U.S. federal income tax system takes these matters into account for individuals! Such consideration will help the tiny church contribute toward denominational needs and ministries in a realistic way that is sensitive to its status.

Finances and Properties

Financial consideration relating to **properties** is not as pressing for the established tiny church as it is for the new one with no permanent land and facilities. The tiny church already organized with land and a permanent structure must allocate funds for the payment of indebtedness and proper maintenance of properties. The new church, on the other hand, must include land purchase and construction of buildings in their decision making. Though such facilities are indeed an asset for the new church, the danger is in pursuing such desires without a proper sense of reality concerning the number of people committed to ministry, the financial base, etc. The church facility is not an end in itself but a tool for the church as it strives to fulfill the Great Commission. The new church might be wise "to start services in a temporary facility and remain there until sufficient stability and strength have been established." Temporary facilities such as stores, schools, other churches, hotel conference rooms, community buildings, and libraries have accommodated beginning fellowships. It is better to endure some of the inconveniences of temporary facilities than to suffer under the agony and burden of heavy indebtedness and financial strain.[10]

Finances and Indebtedness

Another financial consideration is **indebtedness.** Unless a tiny church is provided a sizable grant by the mother church, the district, or the denomination, they likely will not be able to obtain properties (parsonage, land, church building) without some sort of indebtedness. Since this is the case, the issue is usually not, *"Should* the church go into debt?" but *"How far* should the church go into debt?" Perhaps the answer is obvious, but it bears repeating: The church should go into debt only as much as it realistically will be able to pay back during the course of the indebtedness. Ezra Jones states,

> The amount to be borrowed is of major importance to the life of the church. A mistake at this point may result in the failure of the church in future years. Few things are as destructive to congregational morale and effectiveness as excessive indebtedness.[11]

The church people may become so preoccupied with the oppressive financial indebtedness that they lose their purpose and direction. Because mortgage or indebtedness payments are priority items in a church budget, program and ministry needs are sacrificed. Such a price is too high. The church exists for more noble reasons than paying off a real estate mortgage.

Unfortunately, the tiny church is particularly vulnerable in the face of exorbitant real estate and construction costs. Housing arrangements for the pastor, for instance, require a greater percentage of the total income than would be required by a large church, so the tiny church must be very careful in dealing with the issue of indebtedness.

There are two basic philosophies in the acquisition of real estate or the construction of church facilities. The first is financing by assets. The second is financing by cash flow. Excessive indebtedness in the tiny church is usually the result of following the first philosophy. When a church finances by assets, there is no regard for income. The properties are financed by their value rather than by the ability of the church to repay the debt.

Two forms of financing—the bond issue and the conventional bank loan—are available. Although bank loans are harder to obtain, a church may rest assured that the lender will give close attention to their ability to repay the debt. Both past performance and possible future resources and potential will be examined closely.

The bond issue may not have such restraint. Often the maximum indebtedness to which the church will be committed is the total of bonds that can be sold. Such an indebtedness would be supported by assets of the properties themselves but may be in excess of the amount the church is realistically able to afford. The dangers of such a practice are self-disclosing.

The tiny church must take great care and considerable restraint in deciding to go into debt, for unwise decisions here can hinder growth and morale for many years to come. The amount of a church's indebtedness is not the sole cause of success or failure, but experience shows that this can be a significant contributor to the potential fulfillment of a church's mission.

In recent years, public opinion has been that churches are trying to get a person's money. Television evangelism in some instances has perpetuated this "money hungry" image of the church. Money is not an end in itself for the church intent upon serving in the name of Christ, but it is a necessity. As a spiritual institution, the church dedicated to carrying on the mission of Jesus Christ does not see growth or new people as mere pockets of help for the operation of the church. However, a proper approach to finances will free the tiny church ministry in a spirit of Christian love rather than a panic.

Finance is more than paying the bills.

9

When Small Seems Large, Remember...

The tiny church is a significant part of the universal Church of our Lord Jesus Christ, and its value and potential cannot be ignored. For those in the tiny church, however, the struggles seem interminable, and after having "done all," the fact remains that the tiny church is still tiny. There are few people, few resources, and few ministries.

But their smallness only emphasizes the largeness of their task. While a church of 200, or 100, or even 75 people seems large and full of program possibilities when compared to their tiny fellowship, they must not allow such comparisons to hinder their serving the Lord effectively. When small seems large, there are several things for the people of the tiny church to remember that will help them keep a proper perspective:

1. **The tiny church does not serve a tiny God.**
2. **The tiny church does not reflect tiny commitment.**
3. **The tiny church is not necessarily ineffective.**
4. **The tiny church is a proclaimer of the gospel.**
5. **The tiny church faces issues that are often interrelated.**
6. **The tiny church possesses a vision to be reclaimed.**
7. **The tiny church can find God working in it.**

• When small seems large, remember that **the tiny church does not serve a tiny God.** God directed Gideon to select only 300 men to face the Midianite army, and God gave them victory (Judges 7). The army of 300 seemed so tiny in comparison to the Midianites, but they had a big God.

Jesus started with 12 men, many of whom were nothing more than poor fishermen. To them was entrusted the precious gospel that has been preserved and passed on to us. Their group was tiny, but not their God. God provided for the Early Church, and His same grace and provision is available to His faithful ones today. The omniscient, omnipotent God will work through the people who allow Him. That includes the tiny church.

• When small seems large, remember that **the tiny church does not reflect tiny commitment.** In many tiny churches, commitment is greater than in other settings. This does not suggest that the tiny church is holier or better in a spiritual sense, but that the tiny church must have highly committed people to continue at all. Financial giving, for instance, is typically higher on a per capita basis in the tiny church than in the larger church. Members are usually required to give more of their time and effort as well. Many of them could go to larger churches where their personal needs might be better served, but they choose to minister in the tiny church.

• When small seems large, remember that **the tiny church is not necessarily ineffective.** There are some who propose that, if a church is faithful in reaching out to others with the gospel, it will not remain tiny or small. To make such a generalization is both unfair and insensitive to those who have worked hard and faithfully in their setting, even when there were problems beyond their control. The tiny church can be just as effective in touching the lives of people in the name of Christ as the large church. News of the exciting things happening in the tiny church may not be touted, but they can and do take place. If God is the God of the tiny and the large church alike, then He will enable each church to do His will in the setting where each is found. There is every reason to expect the caring, concerned tiny church to make a positive difference in their community.

• When small seems large, remember that **the tiny church is also a proclaimer of the gospel.** Christ did not entrust the gospel to a large, established group of people, but to an unlikely group of 12 men. If the tiny church is focused upon Christ, then it is also a proclaimer of the good news of the love and saving grace of our Lord, and it is contributing to the evangelization of the world.

• When small seems large, remember that **the tiny church faces issues that are often interrelated.** In striving for effective ministry in the tiny church, there are no simple answers, no quick fixes. Though there is little difference between success and failure, concerns or problems in one area will often create difficulties in another. For instance, as stated in chapter 8, financial subsidy or excessive indebtedness can contribute to low morale in the tiny church. A low self-perception can cause the church to underestimate what God can do through them. This may lead, in turn, to a lack of evangelistic appeal.

Many of the issues that face the tiny church are interrelated. The good news is that, in many cases, addressing the issue that most affects that church may lead to greater effectiveness in dealing with other issues.

• When small seems large, remember that **the tiny church possesses a vision to be reclaimed.** When a church is founded, there is a vision for a vital, victorious body of believers that will continue the ministry Jesus Christ began. To plant a church requires hard work, genuine dedication and commitment, and a dream that carries beginning members through difficulties and obstacles. That vision must be reclaimed in the tiny church.

Does it mean that, because the church is tiny, it has failed? Of course not. The dream or the vision, however, is essential if the church will do anything more than just struggle for survival. A renewal of that vision in the present congregation will help them overcome difficulties and grasp the possibilities.

• When small seems large, remember that **the tiny church can find God working in it.** Smallness does not indicate a lack of God's presence. God is working wherever people are intent upon serving Him faithfully. If only one person obediently and lovingly follows God, He will honor that faithfulness. The temptation is to focus on what God does *not* seem to be doing; but when the people of the tiny church focus on what God *is* doing in their lives and in the church, they will begin to expect Him to work in new and exciting ways. When people see God at work, they will trust Him to provide and enable them to minister to others in the name of their Lord.

In that tiny church with the large task, the tendency is to forget the basics of the Christian life and the Christian community. It is easy to forget that God is the Provider. It is easy to forget that He gives gifts to all His people in His church, though the people are few. It is easy to doubt their ability to minister adequately to others when the larger church has so many more programs and resources. At such times, the tiny church can find encouragement in these words from the apostle Paul:

> But God chose the foolish things of the world to shame the wise; God chose the weak things of the world to shame the strong. He chose the lowly things of this world and the despised things—and the things that are not—to nullify the things that are, so that no one may boast before him. . . . I came to you in weakness and fear, and with much trembling. My message and my preaching were not with wise and persuasive words, but with a demonstration of the Spirit's power, so that your faith might not rest on men's wisdom, but on God's power *(1 Cor. 1:27-29, 2:3-5).*

> I will boast all the more gladly about my weaknesses, so that Christ's power may rest on me. That is why, for Christ's sake, I delight in weaknesses, in insults, in hardships, in persecutions, in difficulties. For

when I am weak, then I am strong *(2 Cor. 12:9b-10).*
The tiny church is not left alone in weakness; rather it is God's chosen vessel to demonstrate His power. Those in the tiny church need to live in a spirit of expectancy!

Notes

Introduction

1. The description of the smallest churches as "tiny" is not to reflect negatively upon these churches. This is simply a description to differentiate between these churches and the large category of the "small church."

2. Lyle E. Schaller, *The Small Church Is Different!* (Nashville: Abingdon Press, 1982), 12, 15.

3. David R. Ray, *Small Churches Are the Right Size* (New York: Pilgrim Press, 1982), 42-43.

4. Statistics supplied by the Church Growth Division, International Headquarters, Church of the Nazarene, Kansas City.

5. Statistics were calculated from the District Journal of the 1988 Assembly, Washington District, Church of the Nazarene.

Chapter 1

1. Ray, *Small Churches,* 135.

2. Quoted by Ray, xiii.

3. John C. Maxwell, *Your Attitude: Key to Success* (San Bernardino, Calif.: Here's Life Publishers, 1984), 21-38.

4. Ibid., 30.

Chapter 2

1. Paul O. Madsen, *The Small Church: Valid, Vital, Victorious* (Valley Forge, Pa.: Judson Press, 1975), 32.

2. John C. Maxwell, *Be All You Can Be!* (Wheaton, Ill.: Victor Books, 1987), 83.

3. Roy E. Carnahan, *Creative Pastoral Management* (Kansas City: Beacon Hill Press of Kansas City, 1976), 27.

4. Maxwell, *Be All,* 69.

5. Ibid.

6. Carnahan, *Pastoral Management,* 27.

7. Statement of Purpose, Skyline Wesleyan Church, Lemon Grove, Calif. Stated in Membership Manual, 27.

8. Statement of Purpose, Rockville Church of the Nazarene, Rockville, Md.

9. Skyline Wesleyan Church Membership Manual, 24-25.

Chapter 3

1. Dale D. McConkey, *Goal Setting—A Guide to Achieving the Church's Mission* (Minneapolis: Augsburg Publishing House, 1978), 7.

2. Ibid., 9.

3. Quoted by Carl S. Dudley, *Making the Small Church Effective* (Nashville: Abingdon Press, 1978), 20.

4. Kennon L. Callahan, *Twelve Keys to an Effective Church* (San Francisco: Harper and Row, Publishers, 1983), xvi.

5. Ezra Earl Jones, *Strategies for New Churches* (San Francisco: Harper and Row, Publishers, 1976), 18.

6. Dudley, *Making the Small Church,* 124.

Chapter 4

1. Quoted by Win Arn and Charles Arn, *The Master's Plan for Making Disciples* (Pasadena, Calif.: Church Growth Press, 1982), 11-12. Used by permission.

2. Paul R. Orjala, *Get Ready to Grow* (Kansas City: Beacon Hill Press of Kansas City, 1976), 43.

3. Dudley, *Making the Small Church*, 49.

4. Schaller, *Small Church*, 72.

5. Jon Johnston, "David in Goliath's World," in *The Smaller Church in a Super Church Era*, ed. Jon Johnston and Bill M. Sullivan (Kansas City: Beacon Hill Press of Kansas City, 1983), 22.

Chapter 5

1. Dudley, *Making the Small Church*, 65.

Chapter 6

1. Callahan, *Twelve Keys*, 59.

2. C. Peter Wagner, *Your Church Can Grow* (Glendale, Calif.: G/L Regal Books, 1976), 74.

3. Orjala, *Get Ready*, 56.

4. Ray, *Small Churches*, 153.

Chapter 7

1. Schaller, *Small Church*, 167-68.

2. Ibid., 174-75.

Chapter 8

1. Robert L. Wilson, "Resources of People, Money, and Facilities for the Small Congregation," in *Small Churches Are Beautiful*, ed. Jackson W. Carroll (San Francisco: Harper and Row, Publishers, 1977), 131.

2. Madsen, *Small Church*, 40.

3. Ray, *Small Churches*, 162-63.

4. Dudley, *Making the Small Church*, 167.

5. Ibid.

6. Jack Radford, *Planting New Churches* (Nashville: Broadman Press, 1978), 83.

7. Schaller, *Small Church*, 60.

8. Jones, *Strategies*, 101-2.

9. Ibid., 104.

10. Ibid., 89-91.

11. Ibid., 145.

Bibliography

Arn, Win, and Arn, Charles. *The Master's Plan for Making Disciples*. Pasadena, Calif.: Church Growth Press, 1982.

Burt, Steve. *Activating Leadership in the Small Church*. Valley Forge, Pa.: Judson Press, 1988.

Callahan, Kennon L. *Twelve Keys to an Effective Church*. San Francisco: Harper and Row, Publishers, 1983.

Carnahan, Roy E. *Creative Pastoral Management*. Kansas City: Beacon Hill Press of Kansas City, 1976.

Carroll, Jackson W., ed. *Small Churches Are Beautiful*. San Francisco: Harper and Row, Publishers, 1977.

Dudley, Carl S. *Making the Small Church Effective*. Nashville: Abingdon Press, 1978.

Engstrom, Ted W., and Dayton, Edward R. *The Art of Management for Christian Leaders*. Waco, Tex.: Word Books, 1976.

Johnston, Jon, and Sullivan, Bill M., eds. *The Smaller Church in a Super Church Era*. Kansas City: Beacon Hill Press of Kansas City, 1983.

Jones, Ezra Earl. *Strategies for New Churches*. San Francisco: Harper and Row, Publishers, 1976.

Kilinski, Kenneth K., and Wofford, Jerry C. *Organization and Leadership in the Local Church*. Grand Rapids: Zondervan Publishing House, 1973.

McConkey, Dale D. *Goal Setting—A Guide to Achieving the Church's Mission*. Minneapolis: Augsburg Publishing House, 1978.

McGavran, Donald A. *Understanding Church Growth*. Rev. ed. Grand Rapids: William B. Eerdmans Publishing Co., 1980.

Madsen, Paul O. *The Small Church: Valid, Vital, Victorious*. Valley Forge, Pa.: Judson Press, 1975.

Maner, Robert E. *Making the Small Church Grow*. Kansas City: Beacon Hill Press of Kansas City, 1982.

Maxwell, John C. *Be All You Can Be!* Wheaton, Ill.: Victor Books, 1987.

———. *Your Attitude: Key to Success*. San Bernardino, Calif.: Here's Life Publishers, 1984.

Orjala, Paul R. *Get Ready to Grow*. Kansas City: Beacon Hill Press of Kansas City, 1976.

Radford, Jack. *Planting New Churches*. Nashville: Broadman Press, 1978.

Ray, David R. *Small Churches Are the Right Size*. New York: Pilgrim Press, 1982.

Schaller, Lyle E. *Hey, That's Our Church!* Nashville: Abingdon Press, 1975.

———. *The Small Church Is Different!* Nashville: Abingdon Press, 1982.

Schaller, Lyle E., and Tidwell, Charles A. *Creative Church Administration*. Nashville: Abingdon Press, 1975.

Towns, Elmer L. *Getting a Church Started in the Face of Insurmountable Odds with Limited Resources in Unlikely Circumstances*. Nashville: Impact Books, 1975.

Wagner, C. Peter. *Your Church Can Be Healthy*. Nashville: Abingdon Press, 1979.

———. *Your Church Can Grow*. Glendale, Calif.: G/L Regal Books, 1976.

Walrath, Douglas Alan, ed. *New Possibilities for Small Churches*. New York: Pilgrim Press, 1983.